The Conc

MW00479978

Volume I

Lisa Joanne Flavin

Special thanks to Emily & Allyson, who helped me find the extraordinary in the everyday. And to my husband, Kevin who encouraged me to publish.

Contents

Concord's Scenic Lands and Rivers................ 57

Chapter I

Historic Concord

Ralph Waldo Emerson's Home

Today's musings are in relation to Ralph Waldo
Emerson's House in Concord, MA. It sits diagonally
across from The Concord Museum. If you are
intrigued by Emerson and his contemporaries, it is a
great first stop. Walking the grounds and interior of
the home will give you a sense of where many of the
conversations took place between the literary and
philosophical notables of the 19th century in
Concord.

He was in many ways the mentor and elder
statesman of a group that included Margaret Fuller,
Bronson Alcott, Nathaniel Hawthorne and Henry

5

David Thoreau, however his fame spread far beyond Concord during his lifetime. In fact, the esteem in which he was held is exemplified by the overwhelming response of Concordians of his day to a fire that had nearly consumed Emerson's home. A collection was raised without his knowledge to have it rebuilt.

Emerson was a prolific writer and lecturer on what it meant to be alive, our relation to the natural world, our being. One of his most fascinating essays written in the mid 1850s was on Memory. Two quotes from Emerson's notebooks that I find thought provoking are as follows: "For manners and for wise living, it is a vice to remember" and "imagination is the morning, memory the evening of the mind". Both these excerpts are quoted in Emerson, The Mind on Fire by Robert Richardson. A highly readable, in-depth account of Emerson's biographical life and his philosophy.

Louisa May Alcott's Orchard House

As someone who is from the area, I pass the girlhood home of Louisa May Alcott year round when I bring my youngest daughter to preschool off Meriam Road just beyond Orchard House. Since it is a part of my routine landscape, I find myself only taking note of it when the film crews arrive on one or two occasions throughout the year. However, I chose to shake off the familiarity bred by one too many times up and down the same road and put myself in the position of visitor this past week, so as to experience it from the inside out with my two daughters. Upon entering, I was immediately impressed at how they made the

7

Alcott family come to life for their young visitors. In my particular case, I chose to enlist in a wonderful program called Hand-in-Hand. It is created specifically for girls four to six and draws them into what might have been the daily life of the Alcott children. At the same time it is wonderfully informative for the parents to tour each of the rooms and understand how they functioned for a family of their period.

The high point here was the fact that the audience of young girls were fully attentive and truly curious about the way the Alcott children lived. The program itself was a combination of age-appropriate stories, fact finding scavenger hunts around the house, songs, questions and answers. I highly recommend it. The Orchard House is not a passive historical journey. The people behind the scenes have chosen not to fall into the trap of cliché or standard tourist fare. They have created a living and breathing adventure for young and old and I hope to go back at some point for the "Adult" tour.

The Wayside

Down the road from Orchard House in Concord, is the Alcott's first home, pictured above. This is actually the home where much of the basis for stories of Louisa May Alcott's book Little Women unfolded during the sisters' childhood. The home was subsequently sold to Nathaniel Hawthorne by Bronson Alcott and christened The Wayside. It was the first purchased home for Hawthorne and his wife, Sophia Peabody (when first married they rented at The Old Manse). To say it is a house with character is an understatement. Both Alcott and Hawthorne put there personal touches on it with expansions and updates. The most ambitious may have been Hawthorne's attempt to have a tower built

9

at the center peak to gain a view of famed, Walden Pond. The Wayside abuts a steep incline, providing a dramatic backdrop for its architectural flourishes.

The Old Manse

The Old Manse is a place I have thought about photographing at different times. However, I had yet to take a photo of the place or perhaps avoided it because it is one of the most photographed sites in Concord. Nevertheless, I took the plunge on a day that I felt best revealed its vibrancy despite the somber colors and lack of overt grandeur.

The Manse is simply a crossroads of history here in Concord, MA, a place that saw more than one brilliant mind. Home to Ralph Waldo Emerson and Nathaniel Hawthorne at separate periods in the 19th century, it also welcomed Henry David Thoreau who

11

upon Hawthorne's wedding to Sophia Peabody gifted a garden that still stands active today in an extremely precise recreation.

Sophia Peabody herself was an acclaimed artist of the era and 1/3 of a group of sisters (not the Alcotts) that were at the forefront of the Transcendentalist movement. A great read to understand the landscape of this time through notable females of the period is The Peabody Sisters. Sophia by all accounts a beautiful but frail young women, became a talented artist in the Boston area. Often certain of a short life, it was Nathaniel Hawthorne who lifted her spirits and energized her. During their time at the Old Manse Nathaniel and Sophia would etch their poetic love for each other in the glass panes that still stand in the house today and can be easily read. You feel as if you're looking in on a private moment, while not so unusual in our day and culture, it does, in this case retain a certain sweetness when you see it in person.

The Concord Museum

On your way out of Concord Center toward Route 2 the road forks and in the center is the beautiful ivy covered brick colonial that houses the Concord Museum. The Concord Museum is home to the finest collection of Henry David Thoreau's writings and artifacts. It also includes Emerson's works along with numerous Revolutionary War period pieces. It is a Museum that seeks to engage visitors with hands on exhibitions for adults and children, taking history out of the books or computer and creating a three dimensional experience that people can immediately relate to.

In 1839 Thoreau built a boat named, Musketaquid (Algonquian for Concord River) with his brother John and embarked on a trip he later recounted in A Week on the Concord and Merrimack River. In 2007 boat building specialists reconstructed Thoreau's Dory and photographs of the process were displayed at the Museum. To compliment this theme the Museum introduced a boat building weekend for families where it was possible to construct your own water worthy 18 foot canoe. Similarly, for young visitors, the chance to create a toy sailboat using specifications from the 1864 edition of American Boy's Book of Sports and Games was available as a memorable and lasting token of a visit to Concord; one that created meaning beyond a traditional vacation souvenir. This is just one sample of the inspiring, thematic programs that are created here. Explore the Concord Museum for current exhibits.

Buttrick Gardens, Minute Man NHP

This was the last outing of the season with my girls. A bright, hot summer day and my two partners who have explored the fields, landmarks and shops of this beautiful town for The Concord Life, will be heading back to school next week. So for our last outing we chose to go to Minute Man National Historical Park (NHP) to explore the acres of trails, gardens and views. I was hoping to entice them by suggesting a Secret Garden experience as in the classic children's novel.

This wonderful slice of land and history does not disappoint. While a parent may wish to soak in how the British soldiers and Patriots executed their battle plans along these now pristine fields and waterways, if there are children along, they will be mesmerized by the unending pathways, stone stairwells and ivy-covered iron gateways. Moreover, there are bushes well taller than the average seven year old that have a myriad of trails and astoundingly large root systems underneath. Finally, it is a long journey up to the peak where the North Bridge Visitors Center resides and if you go around back, you will have the lovely opportunity to sit at the North Bridge Cafe that has a patio view like no other. Sit on a terrace sipping ice tea and take in a natural wonder. It's a very welcome sight and break after a thorough exploration of the Park itself.

Concord's Independent Battery

I happened upon what I thought was a period recreation, an early morning gathering of men in uniform and two canons in superior condition. The gentlemen were kind enough to share with me that their gathering was not to act out a prior moment in history but to pay tribute to a member of the Battery who has just passed. It is part of their tradition, along with participation in Patriot's Day and other celebrations, that they honor those who have stood shoulder to shoulder with them in keeping history alive.

This is one of the strange juxtapositions of Concord, one can be driving a 21st century vehicle comforted by a temperature controlled climate or surround sound music and be witness to "live" 19th century tradition at the same moment.

The Battery has been continuously active since 1804. It presently has approximately 50 members, who are the stewards of Concord's proud military history. The canons, they tell me, are replicas. The idea of replicas brought me immediately to present day or at least the 20th century. However, they enlightened me to the fact that the originals date from the Revolutionary War period, when they were active in combat. The replicas are relatively new by comparison, dating just shy of 100 years later, to the mid-19th century!

The Old North Bridge

Tributes to a battle and those who fought in it, made both vivid and poignant through poetic verse. The first, (shown above) I look upon often during my morning walks at Minute Man National Historical Park. The second, Longfellow, is from a collection of poems I was given entitled *The Best-Loved Poems of Jacqueline Kennedy Onassis*.

"It was two by the village clock
When he came to the bridge in Concord town.
He heard the bleating of the flock,
And the twitter of birds among the trees,
And felt the breath of the morning breeze

19

Blowing over the meadows brown.
And one was safe and asleep in his bed
Who at the bridge would be first to fall,
Who that day would be lying dead,
Pierced by a British musket-ball.

You know the rest; in the books you have read,
How the British regulars fired and fled,
How the farmers gave them ball for ball,
From behind each fence and farmyard wall,
Chasing the red-coats down the lane,
Then crossing the fields to emerge again
Under the trees at the turn of the road,
And only pausing to fire and load."

(Excerpt from Henry Wadsworth Longfellow's Paul
Revere's Ride)

Old Hill Burying Ground, Concord Center

For visitors looking to discover monuments from the Revolutionary War the Old Hill Burying Ground dates from 1677 and includes many soldiers' graves from the Battle of Lexington and Concord. It is on a steeply sloping piece of land adjacent to what is now Holy Family Church in Concord Center. If one is looking for a pristine view of Historic Concord Center this is the place to be. On top of the hill one can take in the broadest single view of the many remarkable structures that surround the Town Commons and Main Street. British Generals were said to have set up their post atop this hill during the initial stages of

21

the Revolutionary War in April 1775 but not to oversee victory as they had anticipated, rather, to witness a retreat.

Near the back slope of this cemetery is Bedford Street. Across Bedford Street one can find Sleepy Hollow cemetery where literary notables, Louisa May Alcott and Nathaniel Hawthorne are buried

Authors' Ridge, Sleepy Hollow Cemetery

Authors' Ridge is a place often written about. There are many who have reflected upon it with great insight and historical knowledge. Not presuming to have a similar immersion with regard to this hallowed ground, I wish only to share my observations noted from an early morning sojourn into Sleepy Hollow Cemetery.

The cemetery itself is not comprised of endless rows of headstones. The area looks as if it was carved into the hillsides, one arc sloping into another, dotted with burial markers. The narrow roads allow you to pass on foot or by car and weave in and out of Sleepy Hollow. After proceeding down what are well marked roadways toward Author's Ridge, you'll come to an actual end where the road simply stops and to your right is the Ridge itself, as shown in today's picture.

At the peak of this slope are the family plots of Hawthorne, Alcott, Emerson and Thoreau. While the markers for the family units are of significant size, the individual headstones reflect the character of those who lived. Henry David Thoreau's stone is perhaps just under a foot tall and simply reads "Henry". I have heard it is often adorned with stones, sticks and the like, as it was this morning... a gesture from today's naturalists/conservationists to someone whom they consider to be a founding father of the movement.

.

The Colonial Inn

The Colonial Inn is at the heart of the Yuletide Season here in Concord. This morning, the finishing touches were going up on her exterior. It is a clear, cold day, the crisp air somehow feeling its most medicinal. I'm also lifted by the wonderful scent of chimney smoke rising from the parlor hearth in the Colonial Inn. We are so fortunate to live here, to have the option to stroll back in time like this, soak in the best of what was, while being forever grateful we also get to experience the many benefits of living in the here and now.

School of Philosophy at Orchard House

The Concord School of Philosophy was founded by Bronson Alcott in the latter part of his life. He had been an educational reformer throughout much of the 19th century, his most famous school being the Temple School in Boston. The School of Philosophy is located on the Orchard House property and is situated on the steep incline west of the home. Named "The Chapel", it was crafted simply and exists today in its original form, framed by a magnificent crescent of trees that rest on a glacial slope.

Alcott founded the Concord School of Philosophy as an experiment in adult education to be carried out in the summer. The teachings were inspired by a belief in Transcendentalism. Essentially the concept was that people are born good, that all humans had access to divine inspiration and one could foster a relationship with God through closeness with Nature. The School was unique on many levels, not least of which being that it was co-educational. The principles fostered attracted people looking to embrace self-determination, life-long education and a willingness to include parts of society who felt disenfranchised by 19th centuries mores - chief among these, women of intellect such as Margaret Fuller and Elizabeth Palmer Peabody. Alcott encouraged energetic debate and called these summer sessions "Conversations". The School's ardent supporters included fellow Concordians Ralph Waldo Emerson and Frank Sanborn. It lasted for nine years and closed soon after Alcott's death in 1881. Today, It has enjoyed a renaissance of sorts, hosting gatherings of educators in the summer months coordinated through Orchard House's Louisa May Alcott Memorial Association.

Chapter II

Notable Shops & Storefront Architecture

Walden Street, Concord Center

Walden Street and Main Street are at the heart of Historic Concord. As much as Concord has been able to protect itself from the influx of chain stores and uninspired architecture it has not been entirely immune to outside influences. There is however a deep-seated passion in this town among the merchants as well as residents to rally together when these invaders come knocking. True to town roots that cherish unique contributions, community spirit and a bit of rebellion, Walden Street fought off the most recent "barbarian at the gate", Citibank.

The soul of Concord Center is the quality and diversity of its individual shops. The people who run them day-to-day have a respect for the town and each other that transcends even the natural competition between them. The entrepreneurial spirit is always welcome here, recent shops to make their mark in Concord include The Dotted I and Blue. One of the unexpected luxuries of Concord is the ability to walk into a shop and chat with the owner directly. To know you're conversing with a person who wants to and more importantly, can make a difference, is what makes Concord worth coming to.

.

Footstock Building, Main St.

Well, I learned some interesting trivia when chatting with the Anderson's of Main Streets Market and Cafe last week. It seems in the winter of 1865, the building that presently stands next to theirs, was the National Bank of Concord, Massachusetts. The Bank vault, which at the time was housed down around back, was broken into, in what is purported to be the first major bank robbery in the United States. The robber was a Langdon Moore and the robbery itself was notable because of the method of escape. To intentionally mislead anyone intending to pursue him, Mr. Moore turned around all the horseshoes on his horse's hooves to give the appearance of having traveled in the opposite direction from his actual route. A set of snow prints to cover ones tracks. Pretty ingenious!

Today the historic front of this building features a trademark of many Concord Center stores.... an inventive, custom-made sign in the form of what they sell. In this case, the current proprietor Footstock, displays the silhouette of a boot.

Sally Ann Food Shop, Main St.

Today is another beautiful Spring Day. The view out from my home office window is that of an amazing apple tree, just starting to blossom with pink and white petals. It's Impossible not to be cheered by such a sight.

I was thinking today of one of my favorite haunts in Concord Center, Sally Ann Food Shop on Main Street. It is very low key and also truly authentic. A real bakery that does its baking on premises each morning and throughout the day. Nothing is shipped in from "gourmet or specialty" bakery outlets around the area.

Their breads are amazing as well as pastries. There is just a small table and two chairs inside. Outside is a wooden bench, a great people watching spot in the heart of Concord, especially this time of year. Finally, Bill Griffin, the Owner/Baker is a very nice gentleman and his style and talent sets the tone for the place. If you're in town, stop in for a cup of coffee and muffin or fresh bread you won't be sorry! My young daughter Emily says of the place "Oh mummy, it's so cozy and happy and its smells yummy too!!!" Can't ask for a better review than that.

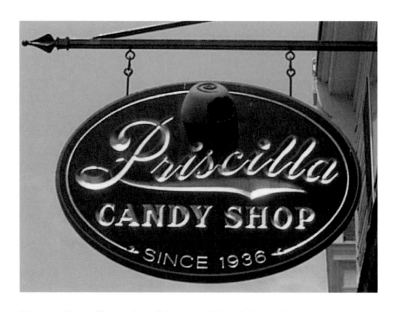

Priscilla Candy Shop, Walden St.

Yesterday my girls and I went to one of their favorite spots, Priscilla Candy Shop. You enter this shop and you get the distinct impression you're someplace special and one-of-a-kind. Upon opening the door the first thing you are aware of is the delicious scent of chocolate. Not over the top, not artificially manufactured to increase buying potential, but the real thing. This place is brightly lit and cheerful. It is not particularly large but gives such a welcome aroma and atmosphere that you must explore further. They have a wonderful blend of toys, gifts and sweets. The items on display are unique and they strike you immediately as gifts one would not find in a generic store. They are tasteful, fun and intriguing. My girls had a hard time tearing themselves away from the small wooden puppets and after some urging from me to leave, en route they found something equally fascinating and colorful. Please let me assure you, although Priscilla's has a creative assortment of cards and gifts their primary expertise is making high-grade chocolates and candy. As so many shops in Concord Center, this is family-run. Priscilla Candy Shop is presently operated by the third-generation of their family.

As for the sign in the photo above, this is a great example of the signs all over what is known as the Milldam District of Concord Center. The style was popularized in France and England in the 16th and 17th centuries prior to widespread literacy. The tradition and actually the law mandating that a sign create a visual representation of what was being sold by a proprietor, was later brought to the Colonies in America. Concord continues to pay homage to that rich tradition through their inventive storefront signs.

Concord Lamp & Shade, Walden Street

I couldn't resist this less than historically reverent mannequin/lamp/sign of a sort that resides outside of Concord Lamp & Shade in the Milldam district of Concord Center. For those of you of a generation, it is reminiscent of the infamous "Leg Lamp" in A Christmas Story. However, this is a classy gal with a lampshade head. So clearly, as pristine and lovely as Concord Center is, there is a sense of humor here too.

The Concord Lamp & Shade store is, for many, worth a trip well beyond the closest lamp store, online or catalog option. Utterly unique, this store can take an antique, precious pottery or heirloom and transform it in their on-premises workshop into a lamp, matching it perfectly with the appropriate lampshade. Works of art are reinvented here into lamps. This has created a loyal following locally and abroad. Situated on Walden Street next to Priscilla Candy Shop, it is worth getting a close-up look at their sophisticated mannequin greeter and taking a stroll through Concord Lamp & Shade.

Fritz & Gigi, The Children's Shop, Main St.

This is simply the best children's shop for apparel you will find. From your initial introduction to what was formerly known as Kussin's, Inc., The Children's Shop (now known as Fritz & Gigi, The Children's Shop), exterior greets you with a refinement and delight that is seldom seen elsewhere. Once you open the door, you know you are someplace special. A renovated historic storefront, you feel as if you've stepped into someone's parlor and the beauty and brightness of the clothing greets you immediately. There is no warehouse effect here. Small rooms guide you from one interesting piece of clothing to another and if you are a parent of small children, your mind slips into thinking about the next special occasion on the horizon that would require a dress or crisp attire from Fritz & Gigi's. I love shopping here at Christmas time. You immediately feel the festive atmosphere and if you didn't have any clear idea of what you would like for your own children or others upon entering, you do before you leave. The accessories are also top notch and unique.

In terms of historic background, my understanding is that one of the three original founders in the early part of the 20th century was Louisa Alcott Kussin, relative to Louisa May Alcott of Little Women fame. She and her husband ran the shop until the early 1970's when their son, Fritz and his wife Gigi took over in their present day location in historic Concord Center. The third generation, their daughters Louisa and Karen, now run the store and to celebrate the store's rich family history, renamed it in 2005 to Fritz & Gigi, The Children's Shop.

The Toy Shop, Corner of Walden and Main

The Toy Shop of Concord is, like so many other shops in Concord, one-of-a-kind. A fabulous alternative to the big box mall toy stores, it resides at the corner of Walden and Main Street. The Toy Shop has been in continuous operation for over sixty-two years and it encourages children to be fanciful, creative, inquisitive and joyful when they enter the shop. The doors open on a world that has beautiful hand crafted European toys, an overhead electric train and dolls of all shapes and sizes. Somehow they manage to blend an inventory steeped in tradition with the "must haves" from many children's wish lists.

The Toy Shop of Concord at Christmas time is not to be missed. Just the act of walking through at this magical time elicits oohs and aahs from my girls especially as they look in the gorgeous front window, home at one time to a stunningly carved and decorated rocking horse. In fact, for birthdays in October, my girls have already chosen an individual morning outing with Mom at The Toy Shop. A chance to stroll through at their pace, not mine and walk away with one special item that is dearest to them. It is the environment as much as the toys found within, that has made this place special for generations.

Main Streets Market and Café

The January thaw was not only welcome this year, it was abundantly clear. After weeks of snowfall and bone chilling temperatures this was a thaw indeed.

There is one place in Concord that beckons people to dream of the Spring months ahead and that is the storefront of Main Streets Market and Cafe. As noted previously, this is a building located at the hub of Concord Center. Situated at the corner of Walden and Main it is a fascinating people watching spot during the Spring and Summer months. Its storefront typifies in so many ways the best of Concord's Main Street. It is warm, inviting, historically rich in

43

architectural details and is the window on some fascinating pages out of Concord's past. In the 1700s this building served as the Town of Concord's Grist Mill and was used to store ammunition during the American Revolution. And while its role in Concord is no longer critical to the building of a town or nation it is still a place that is intricately woven into the fabric of this community for locals and travelers alike.

Middlesex Savings Bank, Concord Center

You can almost hear the hum on Main Street as preparations continue for the Patriot's Day celebrations. The dust and debris that gathered on sidewalks from endless plowing over a very long winter, is now gone. The storefront windows are gleaming and several shops have opened their doors, displaying their merchandise to all those who pass by, in celebration of Spring.

This is a Town embracing its splendor and tradition. Weeks of preparations have resulted in striking red, white and blue banners and graceful half arches over

45

every doorway, window and pillar. The Banks are perhaps the most majestic with their imposing Greek Revival architecture and Doric columns adorned in patriotic color. The picture I chose today hopefully captures just this. It is the Middlesex Savings Bank on Main Street. This local Bank's positive reputation within Concord equals its visual prominence. It has been a major part of the community for decades, promoting the Arts, contributing to the Town and even donating the land for the Concord Visitor's Center.

Debra's Natural Gourmet, West Concord

Debra's Natural Gourmet is a point of reference all on its own. People from nearby as well as out of town visitors flock to its newly expanded store. This place has the owner's personal stamp on all it is and all it represents. During this past summer I started bringing my daughters here to sit at the one long table available to customers, for a snack I can feel good about. The store inside is full of light and with its clean lines and honey colored wood, it is a welcoming place for the serious shopper or the active browser. One almost feels more fit just going there. I find the sheer act of walking through the store reinforces my determination to live a healthier life.

They have a made-fresh area in the back of the store that somehow takes foods, which I must admit would look less than appetizing on their own and transforms them into flavorful concoctions. This includes main fare as well as chocolates, carob and cookies. Also, for the person looking for holistic remedies, approximately half their store is dedicated to this. Perhaps the most distinctive thing about Debra's is the people who work there. They walk the walk and are wholly dedicated to this place and its offerings.

Debra Stark, the owner and operator is one of the strongest proponents of an Independent Concord. Her shop stands in contrast to the larger health food chains with centralized buyers. If you want to know where the food came from, what is in a particular holistic medication or why there are distinctions between brands, the answers can be found where the store resides…in Concord.

Concord Teacakes, West Concord

Concord Teacakes is for me a place to relive moments in time. Rushing, always rushing to catch the 6:35am commuter rail at the nearby train station and hoping I wouldn't be forced to do it without the perfect cup of coffee in hand from Teacakes. Years of well-rehearsed motion: suit, briefcase, coffee and run for it. The trek into downtown Boston and the 35th floor were made a bit more pleasant by starting the day here.

Fast-forward a few years, the rush of adrenaline is traded in for watching the clock slowly tick by.

Waiting for the big moment of my first born while precariously perched in my eighth month on the barstools in Teacakes window. I'm forever grateful for their good humor and extra attendance when my center of gravity was no longer visible.

Family life in full swing with the arrival of my second daughter, the girls and I become a trio with Teacakes as our regular outing. The cakes and cookies look and are mouthwatering. Their whimsical selection of gifts, that are always apart from the ordinary, steal my girls' attentions regularly. And fortunately, my daughters enjoy as much as I, the window on the world of West Concord that Teacakes provides. It is the heart of this side of town. For locals, visitors and trainspotters alike, it is a wonderful place to go and a better place to come back to.

The Concord Shop, Walden St.

This place is not easily duplicated. The Concord Shop has built a very loyal and passionate following over the past decades. It is quintessential Concord in many respects. The Famous Concord Shop has entered the circle of multi-generational stores here in Concord, the second generation recently having taken the reigns. They are committed to providing the best tools for the cooking novice or master; actively seeking out goods that fit their unique offerings. This is not buy-in-bulk retail but a shop run by those with a discerning eye and unbounded knowledge of cooking utensils and all the finer points of what can make a meal a celebration.

When I visited last Fall, I was a bit intimidated by a store completely immersed in the mechanics and artistry of cooking. Never feeling entirely confident with complex recipes and the tools that bring it together, I was eager to embark on a little self-improvement and ventured in. They carry a vast range of items, many imported from France. I found the brightly colored Provence linens especially striking. The owner was so very pleasant, not only was she a wealth of information concerning the variations between the regions in France and how they relate to the designs, it was imparted in such a way that I felt I was all the richer for having listened and chatted with her.

Finally one cannot enter or leave The Concord Shop without glancing up at a sign as unique as the store it represents. In keeping with the centuries old tradition of providing a sign inherently descriptive in its design, The Concord Shop has truly excelled.

Helen's Restaurant, Main St.

There is one place in town that was a mainstay of my youth and now my children's, Helen's (formerly Brigham's). It is a family-run business, as so many still are in Concord, MA. The family has owned the building for many years operating a food shop, later to become Brigham's. In this century, the third generation, in honor of their grandmother, reestablished the family restaurant naming it Helen's. They continue to sell Brigham's ice cream, but have a really nice mix on their menu of hot dog, hamburger fare as well as more inspired, creative sandwiches and other offerings. Very cool interior. Still family oriented but with a nouveau decor twist. My girls love it! A treat after a day at school is going to Helen's. The current generation and the staff in general, are so nice. Really… just the best, neighborhood, welcoming feel to local and tourist alike.

I personally, just love the continuity of things. That I come to the same location that my own mother, who passed away long ago, took me offers a tangible link across generations. The feeling is the same; it's always a good day when we have a chance to take a break here.

Main Street, Historic Concord Center

Concord's array of original shops is the perfect antidote to the sameness of the mall shops a few towns away. I was "forced" to extend my shopping to the malls this December, for a particular craze that is sweeping the 6 year old set. The volume was on high. By this I mean the volume of lights, sounds, fast food, decorations on steroids and just plain stuff was suffocating. The parking lot cars snaked in and out of endless lettered posts, I believe I was finally able to park somewhere by "Y".

We are now closing in on my favorite time prior to Christmas, the final week leading up to the event itself. It is now December 20th and at this point, the office parties are typically over, the race to finish school seasonal events, concerts, etc. is past and of course the week before Christmas pressure to get to the post office is behind us! It is that sweet spot prior to our family gathering where I intend to stroll the shops of Concord Center, Depot District and West Concord at a leisurely pace. I window shop knowing that inspiration will strike when I see just the right gift for the those I'll see in a mere few days.

I'll drink in the sights of this beautiful town just as one might have a century ago. I'll be uplifted by the timeless music, conversation and laughter that permeates this town. My senses will no longer be assaulted by the artifice of the season, but greeted by the sounds of the season; all at a welcome volume.

Chapter III

Concord's Scenic Lands and Rivers

Great Meadows Wildlife Refuge

Positively breathtaking best describes this lovely place, a refuge for people, as much as for the wildlife it protects. Should you find yourself visiting Concord I highly recommend carving out time to explore Great Meadows. I myself had not come to this glorious place before and found it difficult to locate. One would think 3,600 acres of untouched land west of Boston would not be difficult to spot, but finding the Concord entrance can be challenging. Looking on a map you clearly see the large green area, however the entrance is tucked behind a long established neighborhood of houses. The first time through I missed it. Once back in Concord Center, I gave into technology and turned on my GPS tracking to find it. This time the car led me back to Monsen Road just off Route 62 heading toward Bedford from Concord Center; exactly where I got to under my own power. About half way down Monsen Road I saw a small sign, off to the left side noting Great Meadows was to be found on the other side of a narrow drive.

Well, I doubted the vastness of what was in store for me until I parked the car and turned my glance toward an Eden of sorts. I was really floored that something so extraordinary existed just beyond the everyday. When I entered the Meadows itself a roaring wind sailed all around me. My first thought was it had the same characteristics as a wind off the Atlantic seacoast, invigorating and all-consuming. A finely crushed stone walkway leads you through this remarkable place and continues around its perimeter extending into the surrounding woods at various points for further hiking opportunities. These freshwater wetlands serve as a nesting and feeding habitat to a wide range of birds and other wildlife, so dogs and bikes are not allowed. However, come winter it is fully accessible on cross-country skis. "The best things in life are free" never rang more true than in this place.

Revolutionary War Period Farmlands at Meriam's Corner

Today I took a long walk at one of my favorite Concord spots, Meriam's Corner approximately 1 mile outside of historic Concord Center. It is breathtaking in many ways. Trails covered with fine gravel and dirt meander throughout acres of protected woodland, farmland and wetlands. This is in itself is one of the most striking features. The fact that one can experience three such diverse environments in one walk or run is a real gift. The air is absolutely amazing out there. If you plan to explore try your best to breath through your nose and exhale through your mouth. This way you can take in all the varied and delicious scents that come from a mixture of wildflowers, damp earth, sun-dried hay and steady breezes. It is a real treasure! The trail starts at a dirt parking lot where a small bridge extends into an open field. There are wonderful curves and varied terrain on the walk - a great feature if you're looking for a good workout or just a way to keep it interesting. Following the first open field is a wooded area with tall oaks and maples. Then when you least expect, it opens wide into an amazing vista of farmland with the quintessential large white New England barn and Silo in the upper right hand corner of your vision. After a walk of approximately 1/4 mile around the fields you find yourself entering a wetland complete with a wooden bridge that follows the natural layout of the plant life rather than intruding upon it. Throughout this journey keep your ears sharp - this is a bird watchers paradise and there are a multitude of species that sing continuously. When I was here in early Spring, the singing stopped me in my tracks. The sheer numbers of birds in residence and the combined volume of their song is startling after the stillness of Winter.

Verrill Farm

If you think today's picture resembles an American Flag you are exactly right, but rather than paint or cloth the medium used here is a vibrant collection of annuals. Ideally, it would have been nice to take the picture from above, but hills are not in abundance here at Nine Acre Corner, a crossroads leading to the adjacent towns of Lincoln, Sudbury and Acton.

The folks at Verrill have done a great job of growing their farming operation into a multi-faceted family run business that attracts a wide range of people from tourists to corporate sponsors and a loyal local following. Even so, they have managed to stay true to their roots and preserve a farm stand character both in customer service and by serving up a variety of fresh produce and home made products. Also for families or anyone looking for a down-to-earth good time, Verrill Farm has a wonderful year round listing of events that follow the farming seasons, they are a real treat if you happen to be in town. Today was the blueberry pancake festival, absolutely delicious and full of fun with live music and a traditional pie-eating contest!

Hutchins Organic Farm, Monument Street

The most beautiful road in all of Concord is Monument Street. This lovely road may be explored by starting out at the Colonial Inn at the center of town and bearing right. It goes on for about 3-4 miles past some of the most pristine and vast land in this area. A combination of horse farms, rolling hills, lush greenery and varied landscape. This road will take you on a beautiful journey out of town if you're looking for an interesting drive. One spot along the way is Hutchins Organic Farm. It is at the crest of the winding road about half way between Concord and Carlisle. The picture above shows the lands in use and the ideal, pastoral setting in which it exist. My husband and I have sat atop the stonewall overlooking the farm to enjoy 4th of July Fireworks in nearby towns. Spectacular viewing spot on a clear evening! Approximately thirty feet down the road on your left will be Conservation Trails that extend for acres into the woods. Very clear, easily hiked paths with or without children.

The Old North Bridge

The North Bridge has been painted and photographed from numerous angles, but there is hardly a more striking view than that from atop Minute Man National Historical Park at the height of summer. The winding river, sloping landscape and blanket of purple loosestrife frames the famous bridge in a near perfect setting.

There is a calmness that takes over Concord in late summer, a stillness that while seemingly present in this picture, is more likely to be found on the Main Streets of Concord in August. I drove through two of Concord's Centers today, West Concord and the

Milldam District (more typically recognized as the Historic District) and I found it both a happy circumstance and a bit disconcerting that I could drive with such ease through the intersections and narrow roadways. There were just a few people dotting the sidewalks and a car or two occasionally passing by. This is typical August in Concord and Carlisle, where a good portion of the residents relocate to the Vineyard or Maine for a week or two during the summer season and are replaced by those from out of town seeking an idyllic destination right here in Concord!

As testament to this, the serene landscape photographed above, was actually thriving with visitors, history enthusiasts and families picnicking on the expansive green...just off camera.

Walden Pond

Well, I ventured back to Walden Pond to capture Fall in all its glory...crisp air, still waters and bountiful color. As I got closer to the park itself I soon came to realize my expectations were in need of revision. Normally this time of year it's a busy day if you see two or three other people on the beach or hiking the nearby trails. Today, I had trouble parking. Did I check the calendar? Who were all these people with bathing suits on, towels and beach chairs in tow and what is that familiar tune ringing in my ears...an ice cream truck? Well, regardless, I pushed on to see what an Indian Summer looks like on Walden Pond. Actually, once I got by the jolt of seeing a small crowd in the parking lot the beauty of experiencing such a day in October began to sink in.

Temperatures in the mid-80's tell only half the story. It is its own kind of summer day. The children are still in school so the endless sea of beach toys is not visible. There is a calm, joyful spirit exhibited by the visitors stretched out on the beach and gliding through the water that isn't there in the summer. These folks, many of them older, know that this is a gift and one must take in every moment. The water's surface sparkles with such brilliance it's almost hard to look at it for any period of time. It's something about the October rays that creates such a vibrant contrast between water, shadow and light.

So, while this first glimpse made me think perhaps I imagined that the school year had begun and the industrious days of Fall were at hand, upon closer observation I saw the signs of Fall were there, just underneath the warm sky. Maybe this day was a July redux, but being New England, tomorrow it's just as likely we'll be tempted to pull out the wool sweaters and boots.

Concord River

Every now and then when you're driving toward a
destination something catches your eye and your
imagination. This kind of beauty exists along Lowell
Road in Concord, MA and one is hard pressed not to
give in and look sideways, if only for moment. My
daughters and I pass this stretch of the Concord
River regularly on our trips in and out of town and on
this day even they stopped their engrossing back
seat game to look at the color and the "upside down
trees". My close to 7 year old, having completed a
project in art class that looked at symmetry, couldn't
help but comment on the perfect opposite the water's
reflection created and inquired whether I noticed the

symmetry of the two tree lines....1st grade has come a long way since block art and finger painting.

For myself, the feeling this commute evokes stands in clear contrast to the white knuckled grip on the steering wheel that was characteristic of my years trekking into Boston via Storrow Drive (an experience for any outsider). Traveling Lowell Road is made especially pleasant in the Fall by what can only be described as near perfection in its landscape...or as my daughter would clarify with her newly expanded vocabulary...its symmetry.

Heywood Meadow

Heywood Meadow has survived over 370 years in Concord and is a link to Concord's pre-history, as an area used by Native Americans and later to the first English settlement of Concord in 1630's. Its survival has not been without incident. It was originally part of Concord's Mill Pond constructed in the early days of incorporation to power 17th century local industry. Later, The Concord Gun House was built on a portion of it, storing Colonists' arms through the Revolution. This beautiful meadow also served as inspiration to the following century of renowned writers and philosophers. Finally, more recent history of the 20th century records repeated attempts to modify or suspend its existence all together.

Fortunately today, Heywood Meadow is overseen by the Heywood Meadow Stewardship Committee and is a thoroughly protected piece of natural beauty and Concord history. Its full glory is realized in the Fall when this extraordinary Maple that's remained steadfast for countless defining moments in history, reaches peak foliage. My girls and I have laid under it just to see what a 50 foot golden canopy might look like from the ground up. This tree stands alone on a relatively small meadow landscape that sits just outside of Concord Center proper and near the former Hawthorne, Alcott and Emerson residences.

Dedication to historic preservation is a wonderful hallmark of this part of New England. As today's picture so clearly gives testament to, no amount of financial resources given to newly landscaped developments can recapture the magnificence that centuries of growth took to create.

South Bridge Boat House

Once you've visited Main Street Concord and are looking to rejuvenate body and soul you must visit the South Bridge Boat House where you can rent a canoe and travel down the Concord River. The views have not been spoiled by 200+ years of development. Concord has managed to keep the lands that abut the waterway utterly pristine. Birds are plentiful, the water at times resembles glass and the chance to open your senses to the natural world around... priceless. Traveling down the Concord River from the Boathouse can take up to a half day, so pack a lunch. You will wind and drift toward the Old North Bridge where there are several places along route available to bring your canoe ashore. Climb up onto the banks of the Old Manse or further down river, rest your canoe below the visually stunning hills of the Minute Man NHP Visitors Center. This excursion is a wonderful antidote to over-the-top travel fare.

Many summers ago, pre-children, several neighborhood friends, my husband and myself took a pontoon down river for a dinner outing. It was as if time stopped and we all just kicked back to enjoy the long moment. So come next spring, check schedules, commitments and stress at the boathouse dock and step into a memorable experience.

Hapgood Wright Town Forest

Today I traveled into the Hapgood Wright Town Forest a 135 acre parcel of conservation land, the Town of Concord's largest. The landscape is unusual and varied and upon entering there are clearly marked paths into the wood. In winter it's a beautiful and tranquil place to hike or ski. Walking in I was struck by the basin effect that is created by a glacial formation of steep hills on all sides of the trails. The slopes form a perfect frame for the pond known as Fairyland pond. This pond is man-made, however it was created more than two centuries ago. Story has it that it was christened Fairyland by the children of Bronson Alcott and Ralph Waldo Emerson. It's easy to see how they may have interpreted the magic of the place. There is a hidden, intimate quality to it that contradicts how expansive it really is.

If you do intend to explore come in by Route 2/2A East from Boston and at the intersection of Route 126 instead of bearing left to go toward Walden Pond take a right and less than one quarter of a mile down on your right will be a parking lot and the entrance to Hapgood Wright Town Forest. One caveat, this is Concord Conservation not a State Reservation as Walden Pond is. As such, some parking itself appears to be reserved for Concord Residents just take care in finding a place where you can park for a period of time or enjoy a 2-3 mile walk out from Concord Center down Walden Street toward the Town Forest.

Minute Man National Historical Park

My daughter Emily and I took a long hike down from the Visitors Center at Minute Man National Historical Park, over the Old North Bridge, until we were at the river's edge and looking toward the Old Manse. It's wonderful to have such an enthusiastic partner beside me on a morning that was not yet above 30 degrees. The wide-open spaces encouraged us to forge ahead and the cold didn't faze her a bit. This beautiful piece of land was all ours and ours alone. There were no others venturing out at this early and best of times. Our only companions were the chickadees in the brush and the geese overhead.

One can savor the simplicity of this landscape in winter. While Minute Man NHP is abuzz with history enthusiasts in the Spring and Summer, the winter is perhaps the most enchanting time to come here. It is so peaceful that the stark beauty in some ways surpasses the loveliness of the warmer months. Moreover, the very noticeable quiet allows you to hear, see and sense the smallest of movements. Your senses are not on overload, instead they are keener and what you see, while not lush and in abundance, can in a way be more satisfying.

Monument Street View

Stark beauty best describes this valley off Monument Street. The winter sun seems most brilliant on the coldest days, as today most certainly is. While the view itself is supremely peaceful and attractive, I would venture that a walk through would challenge even the hardiest New Englander. The wind whips down into this valley and the snow now breaks under your boot like glass. There is something so strange about a sky illuminated but no warmth whatsoever. I think it's difficult to wrap our minds around what we're feeling because it so contradicts what our eyes our telling us. Nevertheless, it is a gift to have a vista such as this in a suburban town 25 minutes outside of Boston. The mix of town and country here is a delicate one, not always perfect as a whole but in many of its parts, unrivalled.

Resources

Brooks, Paul. *The People of Concord, American Intellectuals and Their Timeless Ideas.* Colorado, Fulcrum Publishing, 1990

Kennedy, Caroline. *The Best-Loved Poems of Jacqueline Kennedy Onassis.* New York, Hyperion, 2001

Marshall, Megan. *The Peabody Sisters, Three Women Who Ignited American Romanticism.* Boston, Houghton Mifflin Harcourt, 2005

Richardson, Robert D. *Emerson, The Mind on Fire.* Virginia, Centennial Books, 1996

www.concordma.com

www.concordmuseum.org

www.louisamayalcott.org

46023327R00046

Made in the USA
Columbia, SC
22 December 2018